Meet My Family

Written by Ronne Randall
Illustrated by Jamie Smith

Contents

All kinds of families	8
Big families	10
Little families	12
Mums and dads	14
Brothers and sisters	16
Grandmas and grandpas	18
Aunts and uncles	20
Cousins	22
Family pets	24

Level 1 is ideal for children who have received some initial reading instruction. Stories are told, or subjects are presented very simply, using a small number of frequently repeated words.

Special features:

Opening pages introduce key subject words

Large, clear labels and captions

Careful match between text and pictures

Educational Consultant: Geraldine Taylor
Book Banding Consultant: Kate Ruttle

LADYBIRD BOOKS

UK | USA | Canada | Ireland | Australia
India | New Zealand | South Africa

Ladybird Books is part of the Penguin Random House group of companies
whose addresses can be found at global.penguinrandomhouse.com.

www.penguin.co.uk www.puffin.co.uk www.ladybird.co.uk

First published 2017
008

Copyright © Ladybird Books Ltd, 2017

Printed in China

A CIP catalogue record for this book is available from the British Library

ISBN: 978-0-241-27521-4

All correspondence to
Ladybird Books
Penguin Random House Children's
One Embassy Gardens, 8 Viaduct Gardens,
London SW11 7BW

Your family	26
Picture glossary	28
Index	30
Meet My Family quiz	31

All kinds of families

dad mum grandpa

grandma children

uncle aunt mum dad

cousins children

Big families

Some families are big.
This is a big family.

How many people are in this big family?

Little families

Some families are little.

This is a little family.

How many people are in this little family?

How many people are in this little family?

Mums and dads

Some children have a mum and a dad.

Some have just a mum.
Some have just a dad.

I have fun with my dad!

Brothers and sisters

Some children have brothers and sisters.

Grandmas and grandpas

My mum's mum and dad are my grandma and grandpa.

Aunts and uncles

My dad's sister is my aunt.
This is my aunt's family.

Cousins

My aunt and uncle's children are my cousins. I love to see my cousins.

cousins

Cousins

My aunt and uncle's childre are my cousins. I love to see my cousins.

We all play and have fun together.

cousins

Family pets

Some families have pets, like cats and dogs.

Do you have a pet?

Your family

There are all kinds of families.

How many people are in your family?

Do you have brothers? Sisters? Aunts? Uncles? Cousins?

YOU are in your family!

Picture glossary

 aunt

 brother

 cat

 cousin

 dad

 dog

 family

 grandma

 grandpa

 mum

 sister

 uncle

Index

aunt	9, 20, 22
brother	16, 17
cat	8, 24
cousin	9, 22
dad	8, 9, 14, 15, 18, 20
dog	8, 25
grandma	9, 18, 19
grandpa	9, 18, 19
mum	8, 9, 14, 15, 18
sister	16, 20
uncle	9, 20, 22